Heinemann First
ENCYCLOPEDIA

Volume 2
Bat-Chi

Heinemann Library
Chicago, Illinois

© 1999, 2006 Heinemann Library
a division of Reed Elsevier Inc.
Chicago, Illinois

Customer Service   888–454–2279

Visit our website at www.heinemannlibrary.com

Series Editors: Rebecca and Stephen Vickers, Gianna Williams
Author Team: Rob Alcraft, Catherine Chambers, Sabrina Crewe, Jim Drake, Fred Martin, Angela Royston, Jane Shuter, Roger Thomas, Rebecca Vickers, Stephen Vickers

This revised and expanded edition produced for Heinemann Library by Discovery Books.
Photo research by Katherine Smith and Rachel Tisdale
Designed by Keith Williams, Michelle Lisseter, and Gecko
Illustrations by Stefan Chabluk and Mark Bergin

Originated by Ambassador Litho Limited
Printed in China by WKT Company Limited

10 09 08 07 06
10 9 8 7 6 5 4 3 2

Library of Congress Cataloging-in-Publication Data

Heinemann first encyclopedia.
    p.   cm.
    Summary: A fourteen-volume encyclopedia covering animals, plants, countries, transportation, science, ancient civilizations, US states, US presidents, and world history
        ISBN 1-4034-7109-6 (v. 2 : lib. bdg.)
        1.   Children's encyclopedias and dictionaries.
    I. Heinemann Library (Firm)
    AG5.H45 2005
    031—dc22   2005006176

Acknowledgments
Cover: Cover photographs of a desert, an electric guitar, a speedboat, an iceberg, a man on a camel, cactus flowers, and the Colosseum at night reproduced with permission of Corbis. Cover photograph of the Taj Mahal reproduced with permission of Digital Stock. Cover photograph of an x-ray of a man, and the penguins reproduced with permission of Digital Vision. Cover photographs of a giraffe, the Leaning Tower of Pisa, the Statue of Liberty, a white owl, a cactus, a butterfly, a saxophone, an astronaut, cars at night, and a circuit board reproduced with permission of Getty Images/Photodisc. Cover photograph of Raglan Castle reproduced with permission of Peter Evans; Ancient Art and Architecture, p. 21; Aquarius, p. 33 bottom; BBC Natural History Unit/Duncan McEwan, p. 39 bottom; Dave Bradford, p. 38 top; David Breed, p. 44 bottom; J. Allan Cash Ltd. pp. 10, 11, 16, 17, 18, 20, 22 top, 24, 31, 34, 43, 46, 47; Bruce Coleman, Werner Layer, p. 38 bottom; T. Cooke, p. 45 bottom; Empics/Rachel Crosbie, p. 35 bottom; Hulton Getty, pp. 12 right, 36 top; G.I. Bernard, p. 5 bottom; Stephen Dalton, p. 4 top; Jack Dermid, p. 28 right; D.G. Fox, p. 9 top; Bob Fredrick, p. 27 bottom; Mickey Gibson, p. 32 top; Chris Honeywell, p. 41 bottom; The Hutchison Library, pp. 22 bottom, 36 bottom; Gerolf Kalt, 25 bottom; Breck P. Kent, p. 39 top; Markus Matzel/Still Pictures, p. 26 bottom; James M. McCann, p. 6 bottom; Okapia, p. 23 bottom; Stan Osolinski, pp. 9 bottom, 14 top; Oxford Scientific Films, Animal, Animal/Lynn M. Stone, p. 14 bottom; Peter Parks, p. 42; Partridge Films, p. 4 bottom; Joe Raedle/Getty Images, p. 26 top; Norbet Rosing, p. 44 top; Leonard Lee Rue III, pp. 6 top, 7; David Shale, p. 8 bottom; David Thompson, p. 8 top; Jim Tuten, p. 32 bottom; Scenics of America/PhotoLink, p. 30; Science Photo Library/Geospace, p. 5 top; Science Photo Library/James King-Holmes, p. 15 bottom; Tony Stone Worldwide/Ed Pritchard, p. 12; David Wright, p. 41 top; ZEFA, p. 48. Special thanks also to Epson.

Welcome to
Heinemann First Encyclopedia

What is an encyclopedia?

An encyclopedia is an information book. It gives the most important facts about many different subjects. This encyclopedia has been written for children who are using an encyclopedia for the first time. It covers many of the subjects from school and others you may find interesting.

What is in this encyclopedia?

In this encyclopedia, each topic is called an *entry*. There is one page of information for every entry. The entries in this encyclopedia explain

- animals
- plants
- dinosaurs
- countries
- geography
- history
- world religions
- music
- art
- transportation
- science
- technology
- states
- famous Americans

How to use this encyclopedia

This encyclopedia has thirteen books called *volumes*. The first twelve volumes contain entries. The entries are all in alphabetical order. This means that Volume 1 starts with entries that begin with the letter A and Volume 12 ends with entries that begin with the letter Z. Volume 13 is the index volume. It also has other interesting information.

Here are two entries that show you what you can find on a page:

The "see also" line tells you where to find other related information.

This is the letter that the entry starts with.

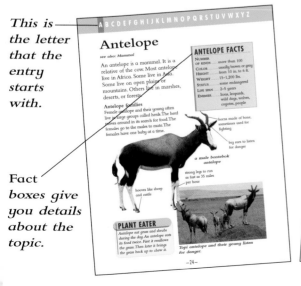

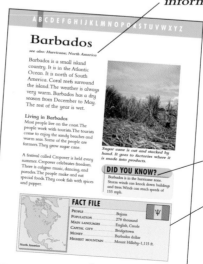

Did You Know? boxes have fun or interesting bits of information.

Fact boxes give you details about the topic.

The Fact File tells you important facts and figures.

Bat

see also: Mammal

Bats are the only mammals that can fly. Bats are found in all parts of the world except the Arctic and Antarctica. Bats make a high-pitched sound that bounces off objects. This is called echolocation. It helps bats find their way in the dark.

BAT FACTS

NUMBER OF KINDS	more than 950
COLOR	black, brown, gray, or yellow
WINGSPAN	less than 1 ft. to 5 ft.
WEIGHT	less than 1/10 oz. to 31 oz.
STATUS	common
LIFE SPAN	15–25 years
ENEMIES	cats, owls, foxes, skunks, snakes, hawks

PLANT, INSECT, AND MEAT EATER

Most bats eat fruit or insects. Some bats eat lizards and scorpions. Some bats eat at night. Some eat at twilight, just before dark.

wings are thick skin stretched between long fingers

claws on back feet for hanging upside-down

large ears to catch the echoes of their high-pitched squeaks

fur to keep warm

sharp teeth to chew food

a greater horseshoe bat

Bat families

Some bats live alone. Other bats live in groups called colonies. Female bats usually have one or two babies at a time. Female bats look after all the baby bats in a special nursery colony. A bat always returns to the same cave, building, or tree to sleep. Many bats fly to a different cave to hibernate for the winter.

This bat is hanging upside-down while eating fruit. Some bats hang upside-down to sleep.

Bay

see also: Coast, Ocean, Port, Lake

A bay is formed where the coastline curves inward. The shape of a bay is like a half circle. Bays are found all over the world in many different sizes. Very small bays are called coves. Deep bays may be used as harbors for boats.

How a bay is formed

A bay is made when waves wear away the land. The water wears away soft rock faster than it wears away hard rock. The bay is formed when the soft rock is washed away. This happens over a long time. The harder rock at the ends of the bay does not wash away. This forms the headland. Sand and pebbles wash into the bay. This forms the beach.

People and bays

The water in small bays is usually calm and shallow. This makes the bay safe for boats and swimmers. Cities and seaports are often built on the edge of bays. San Francisco, California, is called the "City by the Bay."

The arrow points to the Bay of Biscay. It is near France and Spain. The bay is 310 miles wide.

This is a very small bay on the south coast of England. It has a narrow entrance to the sea.

DID YOU KNOW?

The Bay of Bengal is the world's biggest bay. It is in the Indian Ocean.

Bear

see also: Mammal

Bears are strong and powerful mammals. Bears are found in most of the northern continents. Most bears live in forests. The polar bear lives in the icy Arctic.

PLANT, INSECT, AND MEAT EATER

Most bears eat many kinds of food. They eat nuts, berries, fish, and fruit. Polar bears eat seals, walrus, and fish.

BEAR FACTS

NUMBER OF KINDS	7
COLOR	black, brown, red, white
LENGTH	4–11 ft.
HEIGHT	35 in. to 5 ft.
WEIGHT	80–1,700 lbs.
STATUS	some are threatened
LIFE SPAN	around 25 years
ENEMIES	Wolves eat cubs. People hunt bears for their fur.

rounded ears

good sense of smell to find food

strong claws for climbing and digging

a polar bear

thick fur to keep warm

short tail

long legs for running and walking

Bear families

A male is called a he-bear. A female is called a she-bear. The babies are called cubs. A female bear will have from one to four cubs. Cubs live with their mother for one or two years. Then they move away. Male bears live on their own.

A bear's home is called a den. A den is dug in the earth or snow by the adult bear. A mother and her cubs stay in their den during the winter. In very cold places, bears sleep for most of the winter.

A she-bear cares for her cubs.

Beaver

see also: Mammal

The beaver is a mammal. It has webbed feet and a big, flat tail. There is the North American beaver and the European beaver. They live in woodlands along banks of ponds and shores of lakes.

PLANT EATER

Beavers eat the wood underneath tree bark. They also eat water plants, thistles, tree roots, twigs, and seeds.

BEAVER FACTS

NUMBER OF KINDS	2
COLOR	brown
LENGTH	about 3 ft. plus a 1 ft. tail
HEIGHT	up to 24 in.
WEIGHT	35–90 lbs.
STATUS	common
LIFE SPAN	20 years
ENEMIES	bears and wolves Some people hunt beavers for their fur.

waterproof fur is good for swimming under water

small eyes

nose and ears close for diving

an American beaver

large, flat tail for swimming and slapping the water to signal danger

two sharp front teeth to cut down trees

big webbed back feet for swimming

Beaver families

A family includes two parents and the babies that were born in the past two years. Babies are called kits. The female might have eight kits in a year.

A beaver's home is called a lodge. Beavers gnaw down trees to build dams and to make their homes. It is made of logs and mud. The door to the lodge is under water.

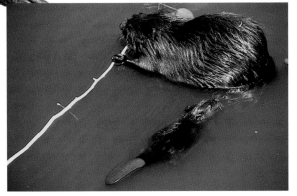

An adult beaver strips the bark off a branch. A kit swims nearby.

Bee

see also: Insect

A bee is an insect. It lives in all parts of the world except the Arctic and Antarctic. A bee makes honey and wax. Honeybees make the most honey. Beekeepers keep honeybees in special boxes called hives.

BEE FACTS

NUMBER OF KINDS	20 thousand
COLOR	yellow, light brown to black
LENGTH	very tiny to 2 in.
STATUS	common
LIFE SPAN	up to 5 years
ENEMIES	bears, honey badgers, birds, ants, wasps

PLANT EATER

A bee feeds on nectar and powdery pollen. Bees find pollen in flowers. Bees make the sugary juice of nectar into honey.

wings to fly forward, backwards, sideways, or even in one place

two large eyes and three small eyes to see all around

baskets of long, curved hair to store pollen

antennae for smelling and touching

a sting to pump poison into an enemy

a honeybee

Bee families

Most bees live alone. Each female bee makes its own nest and stores food. Some bees live in groups. Honeybees and bumblebees live in large groups. The group is called a colony. Each colony has three kinds of bees. A queen bee is a large female bee who lays eggs. Workers are other female bees. They collect food. They look after the queen, the hive, and the young bees. Drones are male bees who mate with the queen.

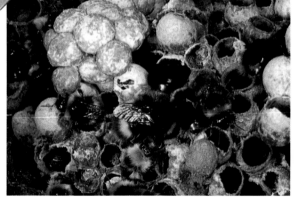

Honeybees make a waxy honeycomb. The queen bee lays thousands of eggs. Each egg is in a different cell in the honeycomb.

Beetle

see also: Earwig, Insect

Beetles are the most common kind of insect. They live all over the world. A few live in salt water. Some live in fresh water. Some live in hot springs. Some live under the bark of trees. Some beetles damage crops such as potatoes and cotton.

BEETLE FACTS

NUMBER
OF KINDS... about 300 thousand
COLOR ..... usually black, brown or dark red
LENGTH .... very tiny to more than 6 in.
WEIGHT .... up to 1 oz.
STATUS ..... common
LIFE SPAN... usually less than a year
ENEMIES .... birds, lizards, snakes, other insects

PLANT, INSECT, AND MEAT EATER

Beetles eat plants and fruit. Some eat insects. Others eat dead animals.

strong jaws to chew through food

wings protected by hard wing covers when not flying

antennae for smelling food

tiny body holes for breathing air

a stag beetle

The dung beetle removes animal waste. It rolls it into a ball and pushes it away.

Beetle families

Most beetles live by themselves. A beetle begins life as an egg laid on a leaf or in a crack. The egg hatches into a grub. A grub looks like a small worm. The grub changes into a pupa. The pupa is where the beetle changes into an adult.

Belgium

see also: Europe

Belgium is a country in northwest Europe. There is flat land along the seacoast. The Ardennes highlands are in the southeast. The highlands are hot in the summer and cold in the winter. There is a central plain.

Living in Belgium

Most Belgians live in towns and cities. The work of some people is making cars and cloth. Farmers grow flax. It is made into cloth called linen. Some people work in coal mines.

Belgium has many festivals. Many of these festivals are held in February. A three-day carnival is held in the town of Binche. People wear bright costumes. The men wear high, feathered hats.

This is the flower market in the Grand Place. It is in Brussels.

DID YOU KNOW?

Belgium is well-known for the fine chocolate candy made there. The chocolates are sold all over the world.

Europe

FACT FILE

PEOPLE	Belgians
POPULATION	about 10 million
MAIN LANGUAGES	Flemish, French
CAPITAL CITY	Brussels
MONEY	Euro
HIGHEST MOUNTAIN	Botrange–2,277 feet
LONGEST RIVER	Schelde River–270 miles

Belize

see also: Maya, North America

Belize is a small country. It is on the Caribbean coast of Central America. The coast is swampy. There are mountains and forests away from the sea. The weather is always warm and wet.

Fishing and tourist boats dock at San Pedro Town.

Living in Belize

People on the coast live in wooden houses. The houses are built on stilts. The stilts keep the houses dry. People away from the coast live in houses with banana leaf roofs. Many houses have hard dirt floors.

Banana trees grow all around. Farmers also grow sugar cane and citrus fruit to sell to other countries. People on the coasts are fishermen.

DID YOU KNOW?

People come to Belize to visit the ancient ruins of Mayan temples. The Mayan people have been here for a long time.

The way of cooking in Belize is called Creole. Creole is a spicy way to cook. It comes from both Africa and the Caribbean.

North America

FACT FILE

PEOPLE	Belizians
POPULATION	272 thousand
MAIN LANGUAGES	English, Creole, and Spanish
CAPITAL CITY	Belmopan
LARGEST CITY	Belize City
MONEY	Belize dollar
HIGHEST MOUNTAIN	Victoria Peak–3,682 feet
LONGEST RIVER	Belize River–180 miles

Bicycle

see also: Motorcycle, Transportation

A bicycle is a machine. It has two wheels. The wheels go around when two pedals are pushed.

The first bicycles

The first bicycles were invented for fun and exercise. They had no pedals or brakes. Riders sat on the bicycle seat and ran along the ground. Then new inventions, such as soft tires, were added to bicycles.

Now bicycles have gears to make pedaling easier. Bicycles are lighter and stronger, too. They are made from plastic or metal.

Why people use bicycles

Bicycles are used for sport, exercise, and fun. Bicycles are much faster than walking. In some countries, such as China, many people get around by bicycles. There are bicycles to carry luggage. There are even bicycle taxis.

BICYCLE FACTS

FIRST	Paris 1791–the first pedalless "hobby horse"; 1839–first pedal bicycle built by Kirkpatrick Macmillan of Scotland
BIGGEST	seats 35 people
FASTEST	fastest ever–166 mph

The bicycle is the best way to get around in China.

This bicycle was not easy to ride. It was popular only for a short time in the late 1800s.

Bird

see also: Animal, Seabird

Birds are animals with feathers, beaks, and wings. All birds hatch from eggs. Birds live all over the world. A person who studies birds is called an ornithologist.

Bird families

The female is often called a hen. The male is often called a cock. Young birds are called chicks. The mother bird lays eggs. The chicks hatch from the eggs. Most birds build a nest. The nest protects the eggs. Then the nest protects the chicks until they are old enough to take care of themselves. Some birds live in groups called flocks.

BIRD FACTS

BIGGEST	ostrich—more than 330 lbs.
SMALLEST	hummingbird—less than 1/10 of an oz.
BEST SWIMMER	penguin
FASTEST	swift—up to 80 mph

A thin beak is good for catching insects.

A sharp, hooked beak is good for tearing meat.

A short, wide beak with a point is good for cracking seeds and small nuts.

The shape of a bird's beak helps it to eat certain kinds of food. Birds also use their beaks to pick up things.

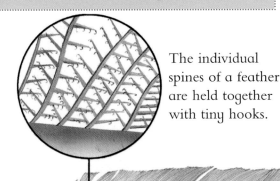

The individual spines of a feather are held together with tiny hooks.

Only birds have feathers, but not all birds fly. Thick feathers help keep birds warm in cold weather. The color of feathers helps birds hide from their enemies.

Bison

see also: Buffalo, Mammal

Bison are mammals. They are a type of long-haired wild cattle. There are two kinds of bison—the European bison called a wisent and the American bison. Bison are often incorrectly called buffalo.

American bison live in Canada and the United States. Once there may have been as many as 60 million American bison. Many bison were hunted and killed in the past 150 years. Today there are fewer than 100 thousand.

Bison families

A male is called a bull. A female is called a cow. A baby is called a calf. The cow has a calf every year. Most bulls, cows, and calves live together in large groups called herds. When there is danger, the bulls make a circle around the cows and calves to protect them. Bison's homes are wherever they are feeding.

BISON FACTS

NUMBER OF KINDS	2
COLOR	brown
HEIGHT	5 to 7 feet
WEIGHT	up to 2,200 lbs.
STATUS	threatened
LIFE SPAN	around 20 years
ENEMIES	wolves, coyotes

wool-like coat on head, neck, and shoulders to keep warm in winter; coat falls off in summer

horns for fighting

good sense of smell to avoid danger

hooves that spread to walk on grass and in snow

an American bison bull

PLANT EATER

Bison eat grass and drink water. Bison used to roam north in the spring and south in the winter to find new grass.

This American bison guards her calf from danger.

Blood

see also: Heart, Human Body

Blood is a liquid. It moves around in the bodies of most animals. The heart pumps blood along pipes called arteries. Other pipes called veins carry the blood back to the heart.

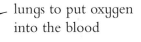

FACTS

A growing child's body has about 1 gallon of blood.

What is blood?

Blood is mostly water and tiny cells. There are millions of cells in each drop of blood. Most of the cells are red cells. They carry oxygen and give blood its red color. Some are white cells. They fight disease.

What is blood for?

Blood carries food to the brain and muscles. Blood carries oxygen from the lungs to all parts of the body. Blood carries away waste.

Blood helps the body cool down when the body gets too hot. The blood moves beneath the skin so that the blood can cool down.

New blood

The body may not be able to replace blood if blood is lost quickly. This can cause illness or death. Doctors can help by giving a blood transfusion. They pump blood into the sick person's veins.

heart

lungs to put oxygen into the blood

arteries

veins

This picture shows how blood moves around the body. The red blood has oxygen in it. The blue blood is going back to the lungs for more oxygen.

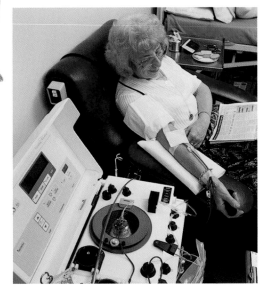

This blood donor is giving her blood so hospitals can give it to people who need it.

Bolivia

see also: South America

Bolivia is a country in South America. The land in the west is high and flat. The Andes Mountains are also in the west. In the east is the low, hot jungle of the Amazon River.

Living in Bolivia

Most Bolivians are farmers. Families grow crops of potatoes and corn. They build small, one-story, mud brick houses. Children go to school and they look after the animals. The animals are usually llamas and sheep.

People in the mountains grow potatoes. They keep potatoes for eating all year round. They squeeze out the water and freeze the potatoes in the cold mountain air.

Bolivians in the country weave brightly-colored clothes. Many native women wear round-topped hats.

Local women wear hats and shawls to the market at Tihuanaca.

DID YOU KNOW?

Lake Titicaca is the highest lake in the world on which boats sail.

South America

FACT FILE

PEOPLE	Bolivians
POPULATION	about 8 million
MAIN LANGUAGES	Spanish, Aymara, Quéchua
CAPITAL CITY	La Paz and Sucre
MONEY	Boliviano
HIGHEST MOUNTAIN	Sajama—21,470 feet.
LONGEST RIVER	Madeira River—2,099 miles

Bosnia–Herzegovina

see also: Serbia and Montenegro

Bosnia-Herzegovina is a country in southeast Europe. It has many mountains. There are forests in the mountains. The land in the north is flat. The winters in the north are cold and snowy. The summers are warm and wet. The south has mild winters and hot summers.

Living in Bosnia–Herzegovina

Many Bosnians live in small towns and villages. Houses are often made of gray stone and have gray or red tiled roofs. People make woolen rugs and silk in bright colors. Farmers in the country grow grain, fruit, berries, and nuts.

Some Bosnians eat *burek* for breakfast. *Burek* is a cheese, meat, or potato pie. A favorite dessert is baklava. It is a sweet pastry filled with nuts, dried fruit, and honey.

This is the market in Bacarsija Tower Square. It is in the city of Sarajevo.

DID YOU KNOW?

Some Bosnians write the Serbo-Croatian language using the same alphabet as Americans. Other people use another alphabet. It is called the Cyrillic alphabet. Its letters are shaped differently.

FACT FILE

Europe

PEOPLE	Bosnians
POPULATION	about 4 million
MAIN LANGUAGE	Serbo-Croatian
CAPITAL CITY	Sarajevo
MONEY	Marka
HIGHEST MOUNTAIN	Mount Maglic–7,831 feet
LONGEST RIVER	Bosna River–155 miles

Botswana

see also: Africa

Botswana is a country in southern Africa. Most of the country is flat. The land in the north is marshland and farmland. Part of the Kalahari Desert is in the southwest. The southwest is mostly hot and dry. It has little rain.

The houses in this village are round. They have thatched roofs.

Living in Botswana

Most Botswanans live in small towns and large villages. Many houses are made from sun-baked bricks. Some roofs are made of iron. The people eat a cooked cereal made with corn or grain. They eat this with fish, bean, and vegetable stews.

Farmers grow grain and beans. There are not many jobs in Botswana. Many Botswanans go to South Africa to find work.

DID YOU KNOW?

The San people of the Kalahari Desert make drinking cups from ostrich eggs.

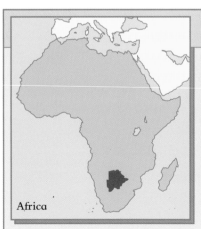

Africa

FACT FILE

PEOPLE	Botswanans
POPULATION	about 2 million
MAIN LANGUAGES	English, Setswana
CAPITAL CITY	Gaborone
MONEY	Pula
HIGHEST MOUNTAIN	Tsodilo Hill–4,266 feet
LONGEST RIVER	Botletle River–230 miles

Brachiosaurus

see also: Dinosaur, Fossil

The brachiosaurus was a very large dinosaur. It was one of the largest and longest dinosaurs. It weighed as much as six elephants. It had a long neck. It was as tall as a four-story building.

Life style

The brachiosaurus lived 140 to 208 million years ago. This was the Jurassic Period. Brachiosaurus bones have been found in Colorado, Europe, and Africa. Brachiosaurus was a peaceful giant. It plodded slowly through forests. It lived in small groups or herds. It spent most of its time eating.

BRACHIOSAURUS FACTS

COLOR	.... not known
HEIGHT	.... 39 feet
LENGTH	...... 82 feet
WEIGHT	...... 33 to 55 tons
LIFE SPAN	.... It may have taken a hundred years just to grow into an adult.
ENEMIES	...... It was so big it had few or no enemies.

long neck to reach treetop leaves

sharp teeth to cut through tough plants

massive bones to hold up its tall body

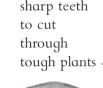

sharp claws for fighting

the brachiosaurus

PLANT EATER

The brachiosaurus may have eaten mostly leaves. It could not chew. It swallowed stones. The stones helped grind up the food in its stomach.

Pendleton Community Library

Brazil

see also: Rain Forest, South America

Brazil is the largest country in South America. The Amazon River is in the north. The world's largest rain forest is also in the north. The rain forest is always hot and wet.

Living in Brazil

Most Brazilians live in modern cities near the seacoast. There are tall, concrete buildings and factories. Many city people live in small houses. Most towns and cities have busy markets. The people sell roasted corn and watermelons.

Farmers grow corn in the northeast. Some native people live in the rain forest. They hunt, fish, and collect plants for food.

There is a festival called *Carnival* in February. It is held in the city of Rio de Janeiro. There are parades. People wear costumes. They dance the samba.

Rubber comes from trees in Brazil. Many rubber-tappers live in forest huts.

DID YOU KNOW?

The Amazon rain forest in Brazil is home to one-fourth of all the kinds of plants and animals in the world.

South America

FACT FILE

PEOPLE	Brazilians
POPULATION	about 184 million
MAIN LANGUAGE	Portuguese
CAPITAL CITY	Brasília
LARGEST CITY	São Paulo
MONEY	Real
HIGHEST MOUNTAIN	Pico da Neblina—9,892 feet
LONGEST RIVER	Amazon River—4,036 miles

Bronze Age

see also: Iron Age, Stone Age

The Bronze Age is a time when people made tools and weapons from bronze. Before this time, people made tools from stone. Bronze is made of two metals. It is made from copper and tin.

When was the Bronze Age?

The Bronze Age was long ago in history. People around the world or even in the same countries did not begin using bronze at the same time. First, each group of people had to learn how to make bronze. Then they learned how to use bronze to make weapons and tools.

Why was bronze important?

Tools and weapons made with bronze are better than those made with stone. Bronze tools are sharper than those made with stone. Bronze can be made into things easier than stone can. Hot bronze can be made into many shapes. Bronze can also be melted into a liquid. Then it can be poured into molds. The melted bronze hardens into the shape of the mold.

Sometimes the people of long ago could not find copper to make bronze. So they looked for a new metal to use. They began to make things from iron.

KEY DATES	
6000 B.C.	People in the Middle East begin to use copper.
3500 B.C.	People in the Middle East begin to use bronze.
2500 B.C.	People in India begin to use bronze.
2500 B.C.	People in Europe begin to use bronze.
1600 B.C.	People in China begin to use bronze.
1000 B.C.	People in Greece begin to use iron.

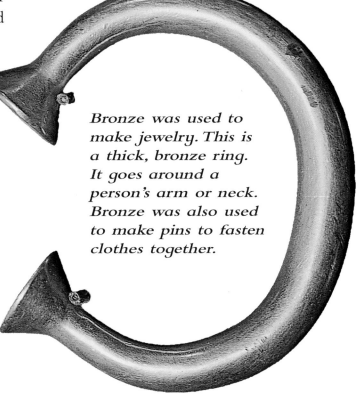

Bronze was used to make jewelry. This is a thick, bronze ring. It goes around a person's arm or neck. Bronze was also used to make pins to fasten clothes together.

Buddhism

see also: India

Buddhism is a religion. People who follow this religion are called Buddhists. Buddhism comes from the teaching of Prince Siddhartha Guatama. He is known as the Buddha. Buddha means "The Enlightened One." It means "the one who found truth."

Beliefs and teachings

The Buddha was born more than 2,500 years ago. He was born in Nepal. He was a prince, but he gave up all his riches. He became a traveling preacher. The Buddha's teachings are written in a book called the *Tripitaka*. Buddhist followers and Buddhist monks study these writings. Buddhist monks are people who live a very religious life. They devote their lives to Buddha. The followers and monks live a kind and peaceful life. They try to always do the right thing.

Buddhism today

There are about 360 million Buddhists in the world. Most live in Asia. They give offerings of fruit, flowers, and incense as part of their worship. An important festival is the Buddha's birthday.

Buddhists pray and meditate at home or in Buddhist temples.

This is the Buddhist Wheel of Life. It shows life, death, and rebirth.

Buffalo

see also: Bison, Mammal

Buffalo are mammals. They are a type of wild cattle. Buffalo are very strong. There are three main kinds of buffalo. They are the Southern Asian and European water buffalo, the African cape buffalo, and the forest buffalo. The forest buffalo is the smallest and has the shortest horns. Buffalo pull plows and do other farm work.

Buffalo families

The male is called a bull. The female is called a cow. The cow has one calf each year. Cows, calves, and a few strong bulls live together in the wild. This large group is called a herd.

BUFFALO FACTS

NUMBER OF KINDS	3
COLOR	mainly gray, but the forest buffalo is reddish-brown
HEIGHT	4 to 6 feet
WEIGHT	up to 1,100 lbs.
STATUS	threatened
LIFE SPAN	around 18 years
ENEMIES	crocodiles, lions, people

horns help in fighting

thick hide for protection from thorns

a water buffalo bull

hooves that spread for walking and running on grass and mud

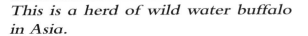

This is a herd of wild water buffalo in Asia.

PLANT EATER

Buffalo eat grass and leaves. They drink lots of water. They eat in the evenings and rest during the day.

Bulgaria

see also: Europe

Bulgaria is a country in southeast Europe. Half of Bulgaria is covered by mountains and hills. Summers are mostly hot and dry. Winters are cold. It is warmer and wetter in the southwest.

Living in Bulgaria

Many Bulgarians live in cities and towns. Some old stone houses have wooden beams. These houses have balconies and open porches. The people eat cheese made from sheep's milk. They eat yogurt. They also eat meat stuffed with mushrooms, cheese, and sausage.

Farmers grow grain, cotton, flowers, tobacco, and grapes.

Tourists visit Bulgaria. They go to the resorts in the summer. The resorts are on the Black Sea. The tourists ski in the mountains in the winter.

These are government buildings in the city of Sofia. The buildings are around a large central square.

DID YOU KNOW?

Bulgaria makes most of the world's rose oil. Rose oil is used in perfume, tea, and syrup. It takes 2,000 rose petals to make a tiny bit of oil.

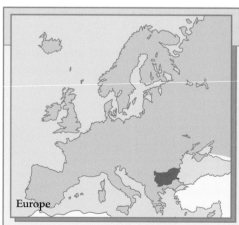

Europe

FACT FILE

PEOPLE	Bulgarians or Bulgars
POPULATION	about 8 million
MAIN LANGUAGE	Bulgarian
CAPITAL CITY	Sofia
MONEY	Lev
HIGHEST MOUNTAIN	Musala Peak—9,600 feet
LONGEST RIVER	Danube River—1,750 miles

Bus

see also: Transportation

A bus is a large vehicle. It carries people. People have been riding buses for a long time.

BUS FIRSTS

INVENTED	France, 1662
FIRST PUBLIC BUS SERVICE	Paris, 1662
FIRST MOTOR BUS	1895

The first buses

As cities grew larger, people needed buses to get around quickly and cheaply.

Horses pulled the first buses. Today, some buses run on rails. They are called streetcars. Some buses are powered by gasoline or diesel fuel. Some are powered by electricity.

This is a double-decker bus in London England, from many years ago.

How buses are used

Buses carry many passengers. Buses are quick. They save energy. They do not take up much road space. People ride buses from where they live to where they work. Buses help in cities. When people ride buses, they do not have to drive cars in the city.

People in some countries do not own cars. They ride buses to make long trips.

Buses like this one carry people across the country. They travel from city to city.

Bush, George W.

see also: Iraq

George W. Bush is the 43rd president of the United States of America. Bush grew up in Texas, but he went to boarding school in Massachusetts. He attended Yale University and Harvard Business School.

Bush in Texas

Bush started his career in the oil business in Texas. In 1989 Bush and other businessmen bought a baseball team, the Texas Rangers. He was elected governor of Texas in 1994 and again in 1998.

Bush becomes president

In 2000, Bush was elected president of the United States. After terrorist attacks in the United States in 2001, Bush focused on fighting terrorism. Bush also sent U.S. soldiers to fight in Afghanistan and Iraq.

George W. Bush is a Republican, like his father, George H. W. Bush.

FACT FILE

DATE OF BIRTH... July 6, 1946
BIRTHPLACE....... New Haven, Connecticut
PRESIDENTIAL
NUMBER 43
DATES IN OFFICE.. From 2001
POLITICAL PARTY.. Republican
VICE PRESIDENT.. Richard B. Cheney
FIRST LADY .... Laura Bush

DID YOU KNOW?

George Bush's father, George H.W. Bush, was president, too. He served from 1989 to 1993. They are not the first father and son to be U.S. presidents. John Adams was president from 1797 to 1801. His son, John Quincy Adams, served from 1825 to 1829.

Bush ordered the bombing of Baghdad, Iraq, in 2003.

Butterfly

see also: Caterpillar, Metamorphosis

Butterflies are insects. They have colored wings. They are found almost everywhere around the world. Some butterflies always live in one place. Others travel long distances to reach warm weather.

BUTTERFLY FACTS

NUMBER OF KINDS	15 to 20 thousand
COLOR	many different colors and patterns
WINGSPAN	less than an inch to 11 inches
STATUS	some types are endangered
LIFE SPAN	a few months to more than a year
ENEMIES	birds

Butterfly families

A butterfly begins life as an egg. The egg hatches into a caterpillar. A full-grown caterpillar becomes a pupa. The pupa has a hard shell. The caterpillar is inside the shell of the pupa. This is where it changes into a butterfly. Then the adult butterfly breaks out of the shell.

antennae to smell food and find a mate

colorful wings made of tiny scales

a goliath birdwinged butterfly

Each butterfly lives by itself. It flies from flower to flower for food. Butterflies come together to mate. They also come together to travel long distances.

PLANT EATER

A butterfly unrolls its long tongue. It uses its tongue to get the sugary juice made by flowers. The juice is called nectar.

This pupa of a purple emperor butterfly is attached to a leaf. It is developing into an adult butterfly.

Cactus

see also: Desert, Plant

A cactus is a plant with a prickly stem and no leaves. Most cacti grow in hot, dry deserts of North and South America.

CACTUS FACTS

NUMBER OF KINDS	2,000
HEIGHT	less than 1 inch to 59 feet
LIFE SPAN	up to 200 years
ENEMIES	desert animals and people

The life of a cactus

Flowers grow at the top and sides of the stem. The flowers make fruits full of seeds. The seeds fall to the ground. Some of the seeds will grow into cacti the next time it rains.

Birds, small animals, and insects eat the flowers and stems. Birds make their nests in the cactus spines. People eat the fruit and seeds of some cacti. Cacti are often kept as house plants.

bright flowers to attract insects

sharp spines to keep animals from eating the juicy stem

thick, waxy skin to keep water inside

a flowering barrel cactus

The saguaro is the tallest cactus. Its huge arms reach high above the Arizona desert.

Calendar

see also: Season, Time

A calendar is a way to measure time. A calendar shows the days, weeks, and months of a year. The way the earth and moon move helps us measure time.

Years

Calendars divide years into about 365 days. It takes about 365 days for the earth to go around the sun one time. In this kind of calendar, the seasons come in the same months each year.

Some calendars use patterns to name each year. The Chinese use animal names. The names repeat every twelve years. Two of the year names are *Year of the Rat* and *Year of the Monkey*.

Months and weeks

Many calendars divide the year into months. There are twelve months in a year. A month is about 30 days. It takes 30 days for the moon to go around the earth one time.

Most calendars divide a week into seven days. The idea of a seven-day week comes from the Bible. The Bible says that people should rest on every seventh day.

DID YOU KNOW?

Every four years, an extra day is added to the calendar. That day is always the 29th of February. A year with the extra day is called a leap year.

September

 11 ETHIOPIAN NEW YEAR'S DAY
Rastafarians celebrate the New Year.

 11~20 PARYUSHANA PARVA
Eight-to-ten-day festival in which Jains emulate the lifestyle of their leaders.

 21~30 NAVARATRI/DURGA PUJA
Hindus celebrate a festival of nine nights of worship of Durga, the Hindus' most important goddess.

 21~22 ROSH HASHANA(H)
Jewish New Year's Day.

 27 HARVEST FESTIVAL
Celebrated at autumn time. Often food is collected and given out to the aged and people in need.

 30 YOM KIPPUR
Jewish people mark the last day of the ten days of repentance. This is the Day of Atonement and the holiest day of the year. A day of fasting.

This is the month of September on a multi-faith calendar. It lists the holidays and festivals of countries and different religions.

California

see also: Earthquake

California is a state in the western United States of America. California has a long coastline and high mountains. It has forests in the north and hot deserts in the south. Death Valley in southeast California is the lowest point of land in the United States. It is the hottest place, too. Earthquakes are common in California. The world's tallest tree, a 365-foot redwood, stands in California.

People enjoy the good California weather at Santa Monica Boardwalk.

Life in California

California has more people living there than any other state. Its cities and suburbs spread for miles and miles. Californians come from many different cultures. There are many people of Hispanic and Asian descent.

Californians work in a variety of industries. They make clothes and electronics. They work in entertainment and communications. Farmers produce fruit, vegetables, nuts, and dairy produce.

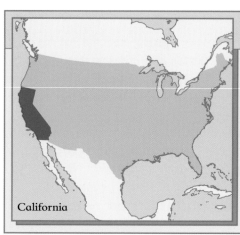
California

FACT FILE

CALIFORNIA REPUBLIC

BECAME A STATE... 1850 (31st state)

LAND AREA......... 155,959 square miles
(3rd largest land area)

POPULATION 35,484,453
(most populated state)

OTHER NAME ...... Golden State

CAPITAL CITY ...... Sacramento

Cambodia

see also: Asia

Cambodia is a country in southeast Asia. There are hills and mountains in the north, east, and southwest. The climate is hot and wet. Sometimes there is flooding.

The Royal Palace in Phnom Penh is where the king of Cambodia lives.

Living in Cambodia

Most Cambodians live in the country. There are floating homes near the Mekong River. Some homes are built on stilts. The people eat fish and meat with rice. Sometimes they add ginger, lemongrass, or sesame oil to give the food a special flavor.

Farmers grow rice, cassava, soybeans, sesame, and fruit. Other Cambodians mine for jewels or work in factories.

DID YOU KNOW?

Cambodian craftworkers weave cloth. The cloth has patterns and pictures of animals. They use thread made from gold and silver.

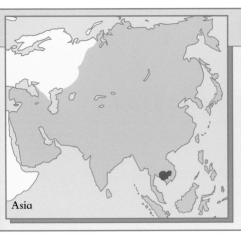

Asia

FACT FILE

PEOPLE	Cambodians, Khmer
POPULATION	about 13 million
MAIN LANGUAGE	Khmer
CAPITAL CITY	Phnom Penh
MONEY	New riel
HIGHEST MOUNTAIN	Kompong Chhnang–5,950 feet
LONGEST RIVER	Mekong River–2,798 miles

Camel

see also: Desert, Mammal

Camels are large mammals. They live in the deserts of Africa, Asia, and Australia. Dromedary camels have one hump. They live in Middle Eastern countries. Bactrian camels have two humps. They live in parts of Asia. People ride camels or use them to carry things.

Camel families

A male is called a bull. A female is called a cow. The cow has one baby at a time. The baby is called a calf or a foal. There are few wild camels. The wild camels live together in groups called herds. The herds wander looking for food.

CAMEL FACTS

NUMBER OF KINDS	2
COLOR	brown
SHOULDER HEIGHT	up to 7 feet
WEIGHT	550 to 1,500 lbs.
STATUS	wild camels are endangered
LIFE SPAN	up to 40 years

large hump of stored fat for times when food is scarce

hair inside and outside of its ears to keep out sand

long eyelashes to keep sand out of its eyes

long, sturdy legs to carry heavy loads

toes that spread to help it walk in the sand

a dromedary camel

A female dromedary camel grazes with her newborn calf.

PLANT EATER

Camels eat desert plants. Some of these plants are dates, grasses, and thorny bushes. A camel can go weeks without drinking water. When it does drink, it can drink 52 gallons of water in a day.

Camera

see also: Light

A camera is a machine. It stores pictures on plastic film or on computer disks. Some cameras take still pictures. The pictures are called photographs. Movie cameras and video cameras take moving pictures.

Catch the picture

Every camera has a lens. The lens is made of glass or plastic. The camera has a shutter. The shutter opens and closes when the camera button is pressed. This lets light into the camera. The light makes a picture on the film.

Get the picture

A still camera uses thin plastic film. The film comes out of the camera and is put into developer. This is a liquid that makes the picture show up on the film. TV and video cameras do not use film. They use CCDs (charge-coupled devices). CCDs change light into TV pictures. Digital cameras put pictures on a computer chip or disk.

Pictures that move

A movie camera takes pictures called frames. It takes 24 frames each second. This makes a line of pictures. The pictures are shown quickly one after another. People see these pictures as smooth movement.

DID YOU KNOW?

A movie film is nearly 2 miles long. It will have about 150 thousand frames.

button

flash

2.1MEGA PIXELS

lens

shutter

a digital camera

This TV program is being filmed outside. The camera moves along railroad tracks so that the movie pictures come out smoothly.

Canada

see also: North America

Canada is a country in North America. There are mountains in the east and west. There are many islands in the north. There is much flat land, too. Canada is cold in the winter. It is hot in the summer. However, it never gets very warm in the far north. Canada is the second biggest country in the world.

Living in Canada

Most Canadians live in the southern part of Canada. They live in modern cities. Some Canadians live in towns and villages. Some people live on farms.

Farmers grow grain, tobacco, and flax on the flat land. The land is also good for raising cattle. Canada has huge forests. The wood from the forests is used for many things, such as making paper.

The Athabasca glacier is in Jasper National Park.

DID YOU KNOW?

Canadian police who ride horses are called "Mounties." Their real name is The Royal Canadian Mounted Police.

North America

FACT FILE

PEOPLE	Canadians
POPULATION	about 32 million
MAIN LANGUAGES	English, French
CAPITAL CITY	Ottawa
MONEY	Canadian dollar
HIGHEST MOUNTAIN	Mount Logan—19,524 feet
LONGEST RIVER	Mackenzie River—1,071 miles

Canoe

see also: Native Americans, Transportation

A canoe is a small boat. It is pushed through the water with paddles. Canoes are one of the first kinds of boats used by people.

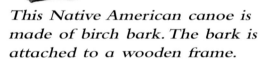

CANOE FIRSTS

INVENTED . . . . about 10 thousand years ago

FIRST CANOE CLUB . . . England, 1866

FIRST OLYMPIC CANOE COMPETITION . 1936

The first canoes

The first canoes were made from tree trunks. The tree trunks were hollowed out. These boats are called dugout canoes. They are still used all over the world. They carry goods and people. Sometimes they have small sails.

Native Americans built canoes from tree bark. The Inuit people of the Arctic built canoes covered with sealskin.

This Native American canoe is made of birch bark. The bark is attached to a wooden frame.

How canoes are used

Canoes are used for sport and fun. Canoes are used in races. Races test the speed of the canoe and the skill of the canoeist.

This canoeist is racing in a covered canoe called a kayak. This is one of many canoe events in the Olympic Games.

Car

see also: Engine, Transportation

A car is a vehicle. It has three or four wheels. It has an engine. A driver and passengers sit on seats inside the car. Energy from the engine makes the car move.

CAR FIRSTS

INVENTED	1885
FIRST MODEL T FORD	1908
FIRST TO BREAK SOUND BARRIER	1997

The first cars

The first cars were slow, not dependable, and expensive. Not many people had cars. Then Henry Ford began to build small cars. He called them Model Ts. People could afford his cars. The early cars had a top speed of 40 miles per hour.

This is a car from the early 1900s. The driver and passengers wear goggles to protect their eyes from dirt.

Cars today

Today, cars go faster. Better engines make cars more dependable. Now there are many cars. In many countries, almost every family owns a car.

How cars are used

Cars make traveling easy and quick. People can use cars to work and shop a long way from where they live.

Cars are useful, but they can cause problems like traffic jams and air pollution. This is a traffic jam on the Golden Gate Bridge in San Francisco, California.

Castle

see also: Middle Ages

A castle is a building surrounded by walls. It is made to keep enemies out. Castles were built for kings and important people. Castles changed over time as the weapons changed.

KEY DATES

1050	Castles were made of wood.
1150	Stone castles were built with high walls.
1340	Small cannons were used in battles.
1400	Big cannons were used in battles.
1480	Stone castles were built with lower walls.

A stone castle in Wales may have looked like this. Arrows could be shot through the narrow windows.

The first castles

The first castles were made of wood. They had a tower built on a hill. A wall was built around the tower. A flat area and another wall surrounded the first wall.

Almost all castles had a deep ditch around the outside walls. Sometimes water filled the ditch. This is called a moat.

Later castles

Later castles were made of stone. They had a tower inside the walls, too. The first stone castles had high walls.

Then cannons were invented. Cannons shot big, heavy iron balls at the walls. The high, thin walls broke easily. So, people built castles with shorter, thicker walls. These were harder to break down with cannon balls.

Cat

see also: Cheetah, Jaguar, Leopard, Lion, Tiger

A cat is a mammal. Lions, tigers, and house cats are all members of the cat family. Pet, or domestic, cats are kept all over the world.

Domestic cat families

A male domestic cat is called a tom. A female cat is sometimes called a queen. Young cats are called kittens. The female cat has from three to five kittens at a time. When a kitten is about ten weeks old, it is ready to go to a new home.

DOMESTIC CAT FACTS

NUMBER OF KINDS	40
COLOR	black, white, gray, orange, or mixtures of these
HEIGHT	usually 7 to 10 inches
WEIGHT	6 to 15 lbs.
STATUS	common
LIFE SPAN	12 to 18 years
ENEMIES	dogs, people

a domestic cat

long tail to keep its balance

fur to keep warm

large ears to hear sounds better

eyes that help it see in the dark

long whiskers to feel its way in the dark

sharp claws to climb trees, to fight, and to catch small animals

MEAT EATER

Wild cats hunt at night. They hunt for mice and birds. Well-fed pet cats like to hunt, too.

Wild cats still live in some parts of the world. They are the ancestors of pet cats.

Caterpillar

see also: Butterfly, Metamorphosis, Moth

A caterpillar is one stage in the life of a butterfly or a moth. Caterpillars are insects. They are found all over the world. They are found wherever there are butterflies or moths.

Caterpillar families

A caterpillar begins life as an egg. A butterfly or moth lays the eggs. The eggs are laid where there is plenty of food. A caterpillar hatches. Then it eats and grows. When fully grown, the caterpillar becomes a pupa. The pupa changes. It becomes a butterfly or moth.

CATERPILLAR FACTS

NUMBER OF DIFFERENT KINDS	200 thousand
COLOR	green, brown, or brightly patterned
LENGTH	less than one inch to 6 inches
STATUS	common
LIFE SPAN	usually a few weeks before forming a pupa
ENEMIES	birds, other insects

antennae to feel and smell

strong mouth to chew through plants

tiny hooks at the ends of legs to move along leaves

fourteen body parts called segments

a claw at the end of each leg to hold food

a Monarch caterpillar

PLANT EATER

A caterpillar eats leaves. Each day it eats more leaves than it weighs. Many caterpillars eat only one or two kinds of leaves.

This caterpillar is fully grown. It will spin a cocoon around itself. It will change into a moth while it is inside the cocoon.

Cathedral

see also: Christianity, Middle Ages

A cathedral is an important Christian church. Most large towns and cities have cathedrals. Many people worship there. Cathedrals often have stained-glass windows. These windows are made of colored glass. The colors make beautiful shapes and pictures.

Early cathedrals

Most early cathedrals were built in the Middle Ages. They were big buildings. They showed how important religion was to the people. Cathedrals were built from heavy stone blocks. The stones inside and outside were carved and painted. A cathedral took a long time to build. Some builders worked on only one cathedral for their whole lives.

Later cathedrals

After the Middle Ages, Christians built more cathedrals all over the world. Some old cathedrals were destroyed by fire or war. They were replaced with new cathedrals.

KEY DATES

1100	First stone cathedrals were built in Europe.
1200–1300	Many cathedrals were built.
1666–1710	St Paul's Cathedral in London, England, was rebuilt after it burned down in the Great Fire of London.
1800–1900	Many cathedrals were built in new cities in North America, Australia, and around the world.
1950–1962	Coventry Cathedral in England was rebuilt after it was bombed in World War II.
1980	Crystal Cathedral was built in Garden Grove, California.
1989	The largest cathedral in the world was built in Ivory Coast, Africa.
1883-TODAY	Barcelona Cathedral is still being built.

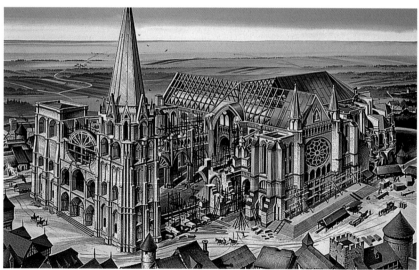

This is a drawing of a cathedral as it is being built in the Middle Ages. The builders used simple tools to make very large buildings.

Cattle

see also: Farming, Mammal

Cattle are mammals. They are related to buffalo and bison. Farmers raise cattle for meat, milk, and hides. Cattle are raised anywhere there is grass to eat. Farmers and ranchers have raised cattle for thousands of years.

Cattle families

The male is called a bull. The female is called a cow. A female usually has one baby. The baby is called a calf. Farmers and ranchers keep cattle in female-only groups called herds. Bulls can be fierce. They are kept by themselves. When calves are able to feed themselves, they are taken from the cow. Then they are put into their own herd.

CATTLE FACTS

NUMBER OF KINDS	277
COLOR	usually gray, white, brown, beige, or black
LENGTH	5 to 7 feet
WEIGHT	up to 4,400 lbs.
STATUS	common
LIFE SPAN	about 20 years
ENEMIES	wolves

tail for swishing away flies and insects

a Frisian bull

strong teeth to chew tough grass

hooves that spread for walking on mud

four stomachs to digest grass

PLANT EATER

Cattle eat grass. In the winter, farmers or ranchers feed the cattle hay, grain, and vitamins.

Dairy cows are milked twice a day. This dairy farmer has the help of an automatic milking machine.

Centipede

see also: Invertebrate

A centipede is a small animal. It looks like a worm with many legs. Centipedes are invertebrates. The word centipede means "a hundred feet," but centipedes can have from 30 to 350 legs. Centipedes are found all over the world. Their bite can be painful or dangerous to people.

CENTIPEDE FACTS

NUMBER OF DIFFERENT KINDS...	2,800
COLOR	brown, red, black, yellow, gray
LENGTH	less than 1 to 12 in.
STATUS	common
LIFE SPAN...........	7 to 10 years
ENEMIES	birds, ants

runs fast on its many legs

two legs on each segment

antennae to feel and smell

an Australian giant centipede

poisonous fangs to kill its prey

Centipede families

Some female centipedes lay many eggs at a time. The female curls her body around the eggs. She protects them until they hatch. Some females lay one egg at a time. They leave the egg alone to hatch by itself. Centipedes hide during the day. They hide under stones, in the soil, or under tree bark.

INSECT AND MEAT EATER

Centipedes hunt for food at night. They are meat-eaters. They eat worms, insects, slugs, snails, and lizards.

A centipede has a segmented body. The segments help it to bend and twist and move through the soil. This female is guarding her eggs.

Chad

see also: Africa

Chad is a large country. It is in central Africa. It has mountains, hills, lowlands, and marshes. Lake Chad is on the western border. Lake Chad used to be very big. Now it is smaller because of a lack of rain and because people use more water for their crops.

Living in Chad

Most people live in the country. The sun-baked houses have thick walls. They have small windows. This helps to keep out the heat.

The people eat meat or fish served with rice, millet, or peanut sauce. Farmers raise cattle, sheep, and goats. Farmers grow cotton, rice, sorghum, and peanuts. The cotton is sold to other countries to be made into cloth.

This woman is selling flour in an open-air market. Grain, dried vegetables, and farm animals are also sold in the market. People also sell colorful rugs and leather sandals.

DID YOU KNOW?

The hu-hu is a musical instrument in Chad. It is made from a bell-shaped, hollow gourd. It can be played like a trumpet. It can also be used like a megaphone to make a person's voice louder.

FACT FILE

Africa

PEOPLE	Chadians
POPULATION	about 9 million
MAIN LANGUAGES	Arabic, French
CAPITAL CITY	N'djamena
MONEY	CFA franc
HIGHEST MOUNTAIN	Emi Koussi—11,208 feet
LONGEST RIVER	Chari River—453 miles

Cheetah

see also: Cat, Mammal

The cheetah is a mammal. It is a member of the cat family. Cheetahs live on grasslands in Africa and Central Asia. The cheetah is the world's fastest running animal. A cheetah can run 70 miles per hour.

Cheetah families

A female takes care of her babies. She cares for them until they are about 18 months old. The babies are called cubs. The female may have as many as eight cubs at a time. The mother makes dens for them when they are tiny.

A male lives apart from the females. He may live with a group of other males. Often they are his brothers.

CHEETAH FACTS

NUMBER OF KINDS....	1
COLOR	gold with black spots
LENGTH	about 3 feet (without tail)
HEIGHT......	27 to 35 inches
WEIGHT.....	up to 160 lbs.
STATUS	endangered
LIFE SPAN ...	about 12 years
ENEMIES	lions, poachers (illegal hunters) who kill cheetahs for their fur

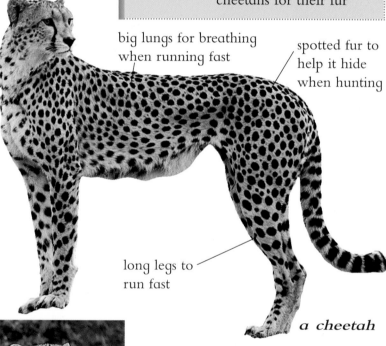

big lungs for breathing when running fast

spotted fur to help it hide when hunting

long legs to run fast

a cheetah

▶ MEAT EATER

A cheetah is a meat eater. It chases and kills animals such as impalas and rabbits.

A mother cheetah looks after her cubs. The cubs already have spotted fur.

Chicken

see also: Bird

A chicken is a bird. Chickens are raised all over the world. They are raised for their meat, eggs, and feathers. Once there were many kinds of wild chickens. Now most chickens are kept by people.

Chicken families

A male is called a rooster. A female is called a hen. The babies are called chicks. Chickens live together in groups called flocks. A flock can have one or two roosters. It may have as many as 20 hens and their chicks.

Hens lay as many as ten eggs. The hens sit on the eggs to keep them warm. The chicks hatch from the eggs.

Many chickens live in cages and lay their eggs on moving conveyor belts. The belts move along below the cages. The eggs are put into cartons and are sent to grocery stores.

CHICKEN FACTS	
NUMBER OF KINDS	more than 200
COLOR	most commonly white, brown, or black
WEIGHT	3 to 9 lbs.
STATUS	common
LIFE SPAN	up to 6 years
ENEMIES	foxes, people

a Rhode Island Red rooster

beak for picking up small pieces of food

sharp claws for scratching the ground

fancy tail of a rooster; hens have straighter tails

PLANT AND INSECT EATER

Chickens scratch the soil. They look for seeds, worms, and insects. A hen will catch flies for her chicks. Chickens kept in cages are fed grain and vitamins.

A newly-hatched chick. Chicks need to be kept warm to help them grow.

Chile

see also: South America

Chile is a country in South America. It is long and narrow. It has high mountains in the east. It has low mountains along the coast. It has a desert in the north. There is a warm valley between the mountains and the coast.

Living in Chile

Many Chileans live in towns in the valley. One-third of all the people live in the city of Santiago. Spain once ruled Chile. The buildings, music, and dancing in Chile are very Spanish. Many Indian groups live in Chile. One group is the Araucans. They weave blankets.

Chileans eat spiced meat or cheese pastries. The pastries are called *empanadas.* They also eat mashed sweet corn called *humitas.*

Farmers raise sheep. They grow grain, tomatoes, potatoes, and fruit.

Farmers travel on horseback across the open mountain valleys to check on their animals.

DID YOU KNOW?

The name Chile comes from the word *tchili. Tchili* is an Indian word meaning "snow."

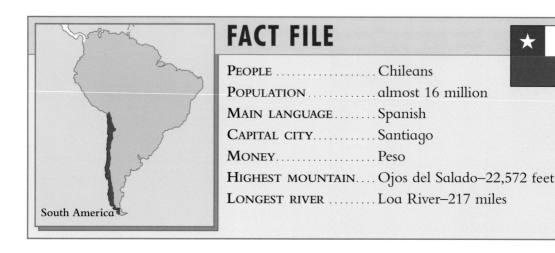

South America

FACT FILE

PEOPLE	Chileans
POPULATION	almost 16 million
MAIN LANGUAGE	Spanish
CAPITAL CITY	Santiago
MONEY	Peso
HIGHEST MOUNTAIN	Ojos del Salado—22,572 feet
LONGEST RIVER	Loa River—217 miles

China

see also: Asia; China, Ancient

China is the third largest country in the world. It is in Asia. The Himalaya Mountains are in the southwest. Warm lowlands are in the east. One-fourth of all the people in the world live in China.

Living in China

Most of the people live in the warm lowlands. There are three great rivers. The people use the rivers to travel around the country.

Farmers grow rice. Rice is grown in flooded fields. People eat rice or noodles with their meals. They use chopsticks to eat their food.

China has many large, modern cities. People ride bicycles to travel to and from work.

Chinese New Year is the most important holiday. There are fireworks. There is a parade. Dancers wear dragon costumes. They dance in the parade.

The Great Wall of China can be seen by astronauts in space. It was built long ago to keep enemies out of China.

DID YOU KNOW?

The Great Wall of China is more than 3,100 miles long. It took 1,000 years to finish building it.

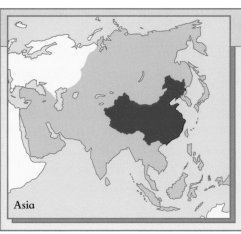

Asia

FACT FILE

PEOPLE	Chinese
POPULATION	almost 1.3 billion
MAIN LANGUAGES	Mandarin Chinese and local languages
CAPITAL CITY	Beijing
LARGEST CITY	Shanghai
MONEY	Yuan
HIGHEST MOUNTAIN	Mount Everest—29,028 feet
LONGEST RIVER	Yangtze—3,915 miles

China, Ancient

see also: China

Ancient China was a long time ago. It lasted from about 1766 B.C. to A.D. 1279. Different families ruled China. Each family's rule is called a dynasty.

What were the ancient Chinese like?

The ancient Chinese were ruled by an emperor. This began in 221 B.C. Most of the people were farmers. They grew crops in fields. They sold their crops at markets. The people believed that spirits had a lot to do with their lives. Later, the people followed the teachings of great thinkers. Two great thinkers were Confucius and Buddha.

What are the ancient Chinese famous for?

They are famous for making porcelain china. They invented paper, printing, the wheelbarrow, and gunpowder. They also made silk. They built the Great Wall of China.

What happened to the ancient Chinese?

The Mongols took over China in A.D. 1279. The Mongols ruled China. They let the people live as they had always lived.

TIMELINE

1766 B.C.	First ancient Chinese dynasty, the Shang, begins.
770 B.C.	Zhou dynasty ends. Families fight to rule China.
221 B.C.	Shi Huangdi takes over all of China. He calls himself the First Emperor.
A.D. 1279	The Mongols invade. The ancient Chinese empire falls.

Emperor Shi Huangdi of the Qin dynasty had this life-size army built of clay. The army was made to defend him after he died.